Can all dec___ ___ ___ ___ ___
through pu___

For Mr. Spoc___ ___ ___
emphatic Y___ ___ ___ ___
place for e___ ___ ___ ___
making a decision?

For Mr. Spock, *Never!*

Even when it's a decision as to who
will live and who will die?

Spock's mind is put to the ultimate
test when he alone must choose
which of his fellow crew members
will be sacrificed and which ones will
survive to tell the incredible story
of...

THE GALILEO 7

OTHER **STAR TREK FOTONOVELS**™
YOU WILL ENJOY—

THE CITY ON THE EDGE OF FOREVER
WHERE NO MAN HAS GONE BEFORE
THE TROUBLE WITH TRIBBLES
A TASTE OF ARMAGEDDON
METAMORPHOSIS
ALL OUR YESTERDAYS

STAR TREK ™*

THE GALILEO SEVEN

written by **OLIVER CRAWFORD**
and **S. BAR-DAVID**

adapted from the television series
created by **GENE RODDENBERRY**

RLI: $\dfrac{\text{VLM 6 (VLR 5–7)}}{\text{IL 5+}}$

THE GALILEO 7
A Bantam Book / May 1978

Designed and produced by
Michael Parrish, Los Angeles

Star Trek™ *designates a trademark of*
Paramount Pictures Corporation.

Fotonovel™ *designates a trademark of*
Mandala Productions.

ISBN 0-553-12017-4

Published simultaneously in the United States and Canada

Bantam Books are published by Bantam Books, Inc. Its trade-mark, consisting of the words "Bantam Books" and the por-trayal of a bantam, is registered in the United States Patent Office and in other countries. Marca Registrada. Bantam Books, Inc., 666 Fifth Avenue, New York, New York 10019.

PRINTED IN THE UNITED STATES OF AMERICA

0 9 8 7 6 5 4 3 2 1

Dear Readers,

We are extremely pleased that so many of you have bothered to write and tell us how much you are enjoying our Star Trek Fotonovels. On the next few pages you will find some representative letters.

Though each of your comments are unique, we do find one question cropping up quite often: "How many Star Trek Fotonovels do you plan to publish?" The answer to that question is wholly dependent on you, our readers. As long as our books continue to sell, we will be pleased to continue publishing them.

We welcome your comments, suggestions and questions. Please address them to:

Mandala Productions
8833 Sunset Blvd.
Suite 403
Los Angeles, CA 90069

If you would like us to consider printing your letter in one of our future books, please include permission in writing.

Best Regards,
Mandala Productions

Dear Sirs,

I have just acquired copies of "Star Trek" Fotonovels #1 and #2. Hurrah! These books are almost as good as having video tapes. No longer do I need to attempt photographing from my TV set (disaster—black bars across everything). No longer do I have to take frantic notes re: what shirt Kirk was wearing or when Spock would let a half smile creep through, or try to remember the fantastically expressive face of Shatner.

Please, please do all 79 episodes...I want every episode as it comes off the press. Yours with great anticipation—
Willa Mekeel, R N, B S
Hopewell Junction, New York
Mother and grandmother
to nine other Trekkies

Dear Mandala,

Thank you for introducing me to a whole new world. Somehow I had never watched "Star Trek" before, but after reading a few of your exciting Fotonovels, I realized what I had missed. Now I find myself rushing home every day to catch the "Star Trek" reruns. I'm sure most of the people that buy your books are old fans who are thrilled to see their heroes again. But I plan to buy them just to get better acquainted.

Sincerely,
Terry Kaplan
Chicago, Illinois

Dear Sirs,

I am writing to compliment you on the interesting publishing format you are pioneering. As a college instructor of Television and Film, I think I may be able to use your books as a teaching aid. Throughout the course of study, my students read many scripts and it is often quite difficult for the beginning reader to visualize what the writer intends. With one of your books alongside them as they read the script, however, they will actually be able to see what a "long shot" is, for example, or an "insert", instead of just imagining it. I look forward to your up-coming books.

Sincerely,
George Bowden
Los Angeles City Colleges
Radio, TV, Film Department

Greetings from England,

As an English TV producer and Sci-Fi fan, I have followed "Star Trek" from its earliest beginnings. The adventures of Captain Kirk and the crew of the *Enterprise* can only be described as Classic American Television.

Recently, while working in the U.S. on a new movie, I discovered your Fotonovels and bought a large supply to take back to England for all my friends. I really thought I had found something unique. Imagine my surprise when I found your books are available here!

I have to admit that when I first heard of your books I thought they would be yet another exploitation of a great TV show. Thank goodness, I was wrong. The quality of the color photography and design are exceptional. The entire presentation is first class. Congrats to you, Mandala. I feel you have equalled the original concept, if not added to it. Live long and prosper.

Vanessa Greene
B.G. Productions

I recently purchased your first two Fotonovels. In my opinion this has to be just about the greatest innovation in publishing history. I have almost everything published on "Star Trek" and I will admit that your Fotonovels are the highlight of my collection.

Respectfully,
Pax Quigley
Palo Alto, California

Dear Sir,

I would like to congratulate and thank you for the publishing of the "Star Trek" Fotonovels. There are a number of reasons why I am so enthusiastic about this publishing attempt.

First, there are a large number of very enthusiastic "Star Trek" fans who will purchase almost anything connected with this television series.

Second, there are a large number of Science Fiction fans in general who are fascinated to actually see their own dreams of space travel to other planets and contact with other civilizations captured in both pictures and words. To be able to abandon one's daily worries by losing oneself in the world of a "Star Trek" Fotonovel is an experience similar to that experienced by moviegoers to "Star Wars."

Third, many of us failed to see the original series in color.

Fourth, the Fotonovels are excellently produced. The scenes capture very critical facial expressions of the actors, plus the amazing scenic backgrounds.

Sincerely yours,
Stephen D. Shaffer
Ph.D. Candidate
Ohio State University

CAST LIST
On board the *Enterprise:*

James T. Kirk, Captain
William Shatner

A man whose independent nature and compassionate heart make him a natural leader. His overriding concern is always the well-being of his ship and its crew which earns him their undying respect and love.

Mr. Ferris, High Commissioner
John Crawford

The overzealous Federation official who will stop at nothing in order to insure his mission's success.

Uhura, Lt., Communications Officer
Nichelle Nichols

Sulu, Chief Helmsman
George Takei

Kelowitz, Lt. Commander
Grant Woods

Transporter Officer
David L. Ross

On board the *Galileo:*

Spock, First Officer
Leonard Nimoy

Of Vulcan and Terran heritage, which accounts for his analytical mind and extraordinary strength. Logic and reason rule his life.

Leonard McCoy, M.D., Lt. Commander
DeForest Kelley

Senior Ship's Surgeon, head of Life Sciences Department. Though surrounded by the most advanced equipment the 24th Century can offer, he still practices medicine more with his heart than his head.

Montgomery Scott, Lt. Commander
James Doohan

Chief Engineer. Unchallenged in his knowledge of the ship's engineering equipment. A veritable magician when it comes to seemingly impossible repairs.

Boma,
Lieutenant
Don Marshall

Gaetano,
Lieutenant
Peter Marko

Latimer,
Lieutenant
Reese Vaughn

Mears,
Yeoman
Phyllis Douglas

THE
GALILEO
SEVEN

SPACE:

THE FINAL FRONTIER

THESE ARE THE VOYAGES OF
THE STARSHIP "ENTERPRISE."
ITS FIVE YEAR MISSION:
TO EXPLORE STRANGE NEW
WORLDS . . . TO SEEK OUT NEW LIFE
AND NEW CIVILIZATIONS . . .
TO BOLDLY GO WHERE
NO MAN HAS GONE BEFORE.

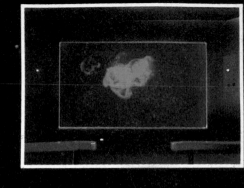

CAPTAIN'S LOG

STARDATE 2821.5

EN ROUTE TO MAKUS III
WITH A CARGO OF MEDICAL
SUPPLIES. OUR COURSE
LEADS US PAST MURASAKI
312, A QUASAR-LIKE FOR-
MATION . . . VAGUE . . .
UNDEFINED . . . A PRICE-
LESS OPPORTUNITY FOR
SCIENTIFIC INVESTIGA-
TION. ON BOARD IS GALAC-
TIC HIGH COMMISSIONER
FERRIS, OVERSEEING THE
DELIVERY OF MEDICINES
TO MAKUS III.

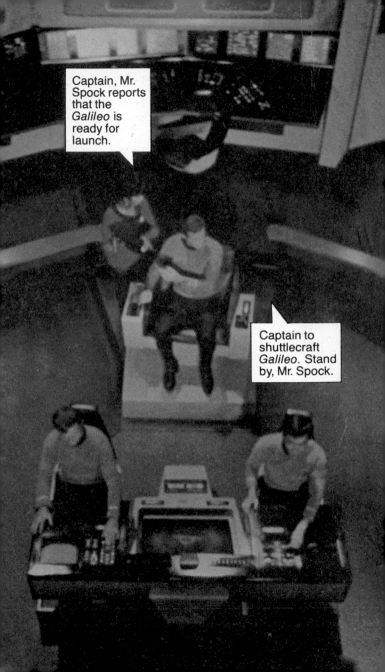

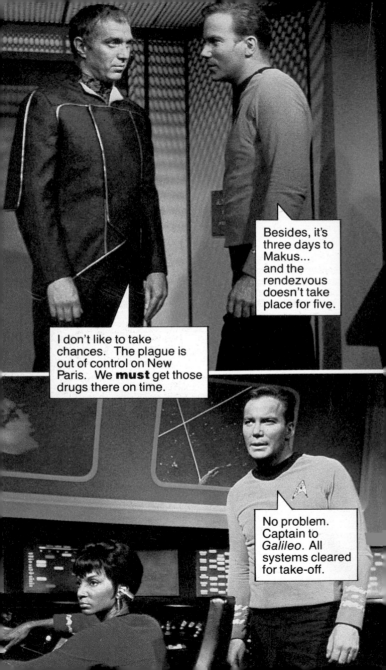

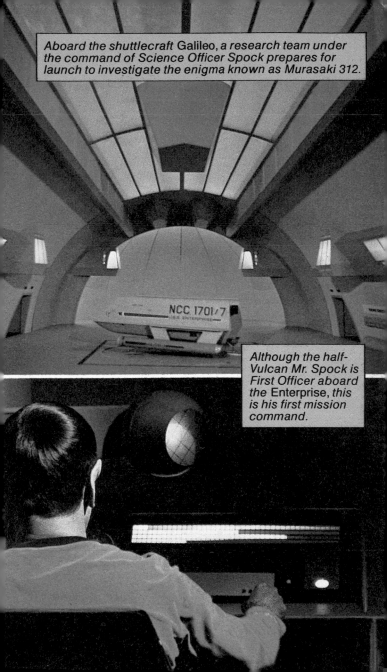

Aboard the shuttlecraft Galileo, a research team under the command of Science Officer Spock prepares for launch to investigate the enigma known as Murasaki 312.

Although the half-Vulcan Mr. Spock is First Officer aboard the Enterprise, this is his first mission command.

Power up. All instruments activated. All readings normal. All go.

Launch shuttlecraft.

In launch mode, the seven aboard the Galileo await the smooth opening of the great doors of the hangar deck at the stern of the secondary hull.

There is a saying in Star Fleet regarding shuttlecraft exits: No matter how many times you've done it, you never lose a feeling of reverence as the awesome spectacle of space opens before you.

Inside the shuttlecraft, Science Officer Spock, Engineering Officer Scott, Ship's Surgeon McCoy, Lieutenants Boma, Gaetano and Latimer, and Yeoman Mears head toward what they believe to be a routine scientific survey.

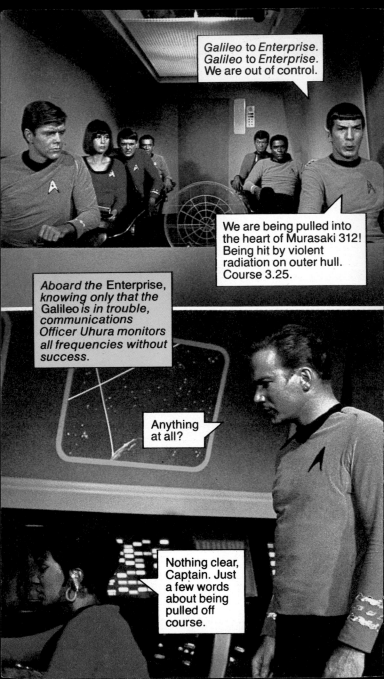

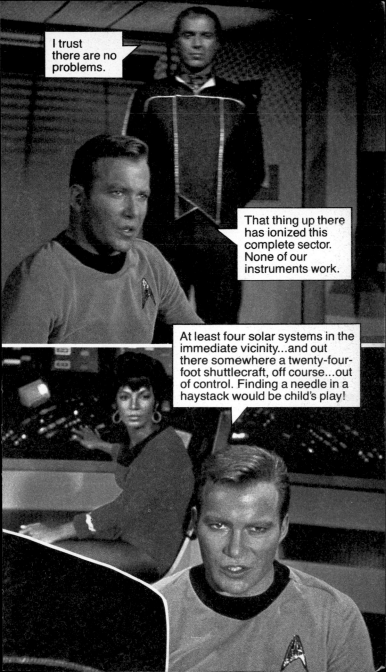

CAPTAIN'S LOG

STARDATE 2821.7

EFFORTS TO CONTACT THE TEAM ABOARD THE SHUTTLECRAFT "GALILEO" ARE THWARTED BY INSTRUMENT DYSFUNCTION DUE TO THE MURASAKI EFFECT. WE HAVE HAD NO REAL COMMUNICATION FROM THEM SINCE JUST PRIOR TO LAUNCH. ALL WE DO KNOW IS THAT THEY HAVE BEEN PULLED OFF COURSE. HOW FAR IS ANYONE'S GUESS.

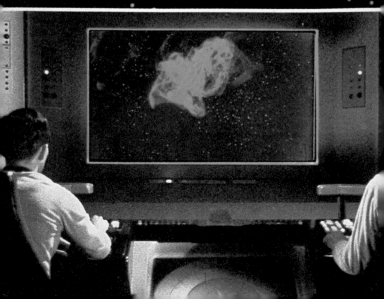

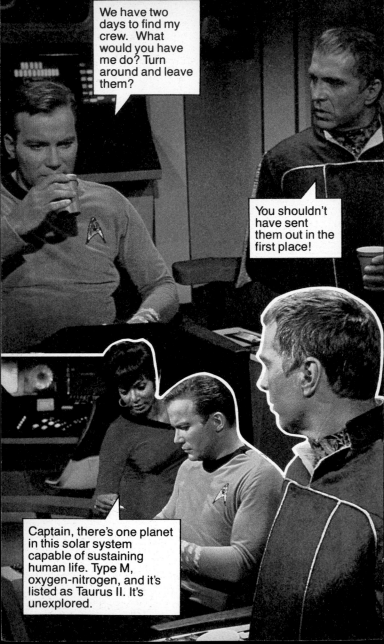

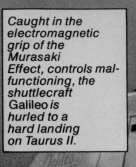

Caught in the electromagnetic grip of the Murasaki Effect, controls malfunctioning, the shuttlecraft *Galileo* is hurled to a hard landing on Taurus II.

NCC-17
U.S.S. ENTERPR

Dazed and shaken, the crew assess their situation.

Are you all right?

Yes, just a bruise or two.

I just got a little bump on the head.

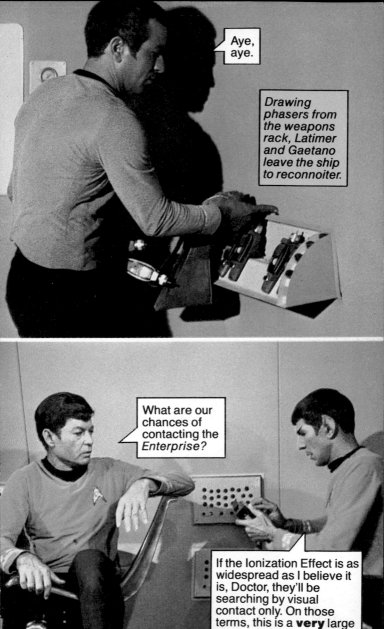

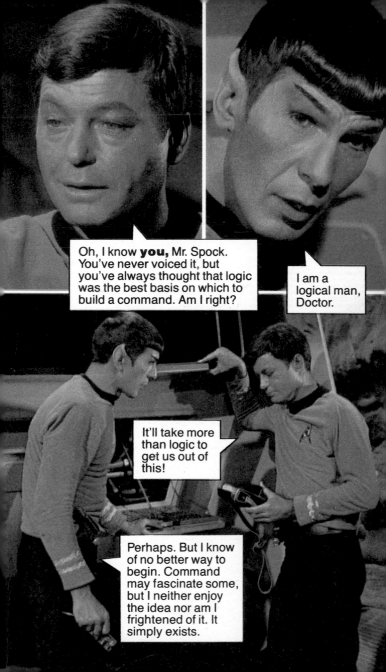

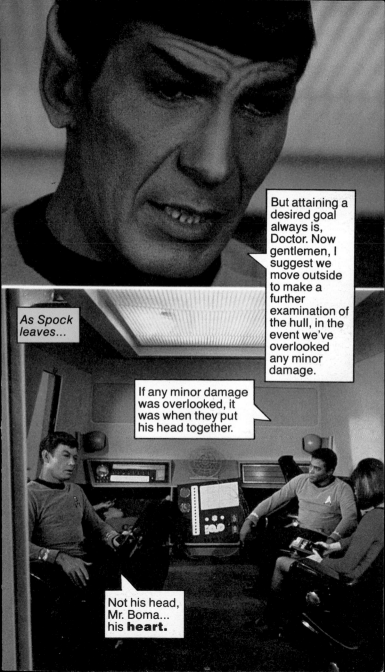

Scouting near-by, Gaetano and Latimer are alerted by a rasping, shuffling sound from a source impossible to pinpoint in the swirling mist.
What is it?
I don't know. It's from up there.
No...no... it's from back there.
It's **everywhere**— all around us!

Apprehensive, Latimer and Gaetano make their way toward the shuttlecraft, unable to shake a sense of foreboding.

Straining to penetrate the drifting haze, they can see nothing but the rocky, alien terrain.

On a ledge above, a figure waits for them to come within range. The heavy spear is lifted...and cast with angry force...

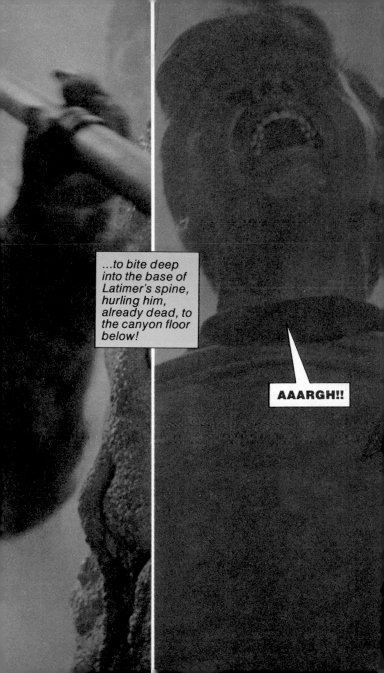

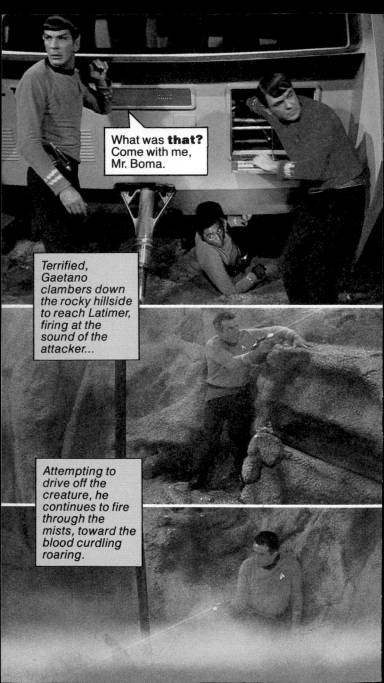

CAPTAIN'S LOG

STARDATE 2822.3

THE ELECTROMAGNETIC
PHENOMENON KNOWN AS
MURASAKI 312 WHIRLS
LIKE SOME ANGRY BLIGHT
IN SPACE. A DEPRESSING
REMINDER THAT SEVEN OF
OUR SHIPMATES STILL
HAVE NOT BEEN HEARD
FROM. EQUALLY BAD, THE
EFFECT HAS RENDERED OUR
NORMAL SEARCHING SYS-
TEMS USELESS. WITHOUT
THEM, WE ARE BLIND AND
ALMOST HELPLESS.

Captain, the *Columbus* has returned from searching Quadrant 779 X by 534 M. Results: negative.

Have them proceed on to the next quadrants. Any word from Engineering on our sensors?

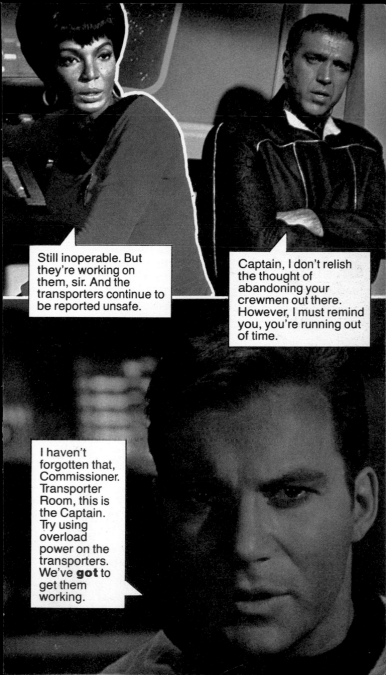

On Taurus II, Latimer's death has left the Galileo *still three hundred pounds over lift-off weight. In desperation, the crew rip out every nonessential item, while Scotty works on, against hopeless odds.*

This should save us at least fifty pounds, Mr. Spock, and we should be able to scrape up another hundred pounds.

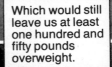

Which would still leave us at least one hundred and fifty pounds overweight.

Perhaps if you were to channel the second auxiliary tank through the primary intake valve...

It's too delicate. It may not be able to take the pressure as it is.

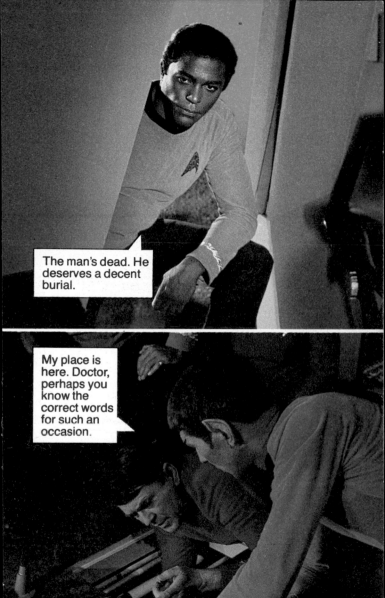

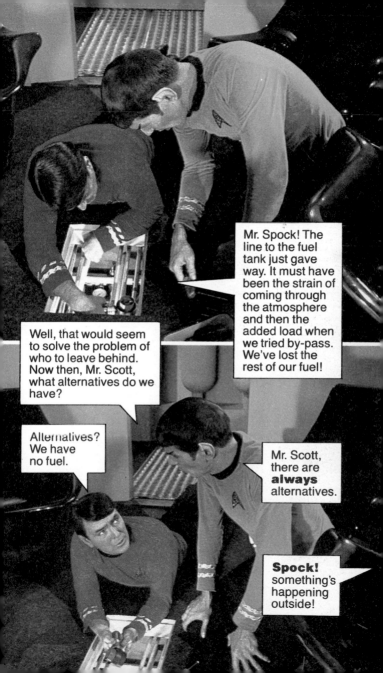

It seems **logical** to me.
Yes indeed. It seems logical to me also. But to take life **indiscriminately...**

Gentlemen, you will follow my orders to the letter, firing only when so instructed and at my designated targets.

Now you're talking! ...You saw what they did to Latimer.

We'll fire to frighten, Mr. Gaetano. Not to kill. Follow me.

Theorizing that a mild show of force will keep the attackers at bay until the Galileo can achieve lift-off, Spock, Boma and Gaetano return to the place where Latimer was killed.

The ominous rasping sound through the harsh landscape is the only evidence of the creatures, until the mists part enough to reveal a huge spear and shield on a rocky ledge ahead.

A hail of spears, cast from the cliffs, falls among them, narrowly missing them. His phaser set to stun, Spock fires at one of the brutes, now dimly visible on the fog shrouded ledge above.

The shaggy beast's fearful growling resounds through the canyon as it takes the phaser hit on its primitive shield...

Leaping to a vantage point on the rocks, Spock weighs the moment... and gives the order.

Fire!

Resisting the urge to fire wildly all about them, Boma and Gaetano remain steadfast, and fire as directed...

The unearthly howling diminishes, and seems to recede in the haze.

Cease firing. They should think twice before bothering us again.

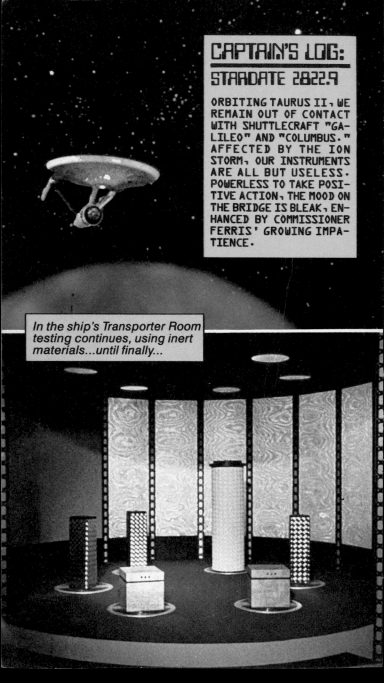

CAPTAIN'S LOG:

STARDATE 2822.9

ORBITING TAURUS II, WE REMAIN OUT OF CONTACT WITH SHUTTLECRAFT "GALILEO" AND "COLUMBUS." AFFECTED BY THE ION STORM, OUR INSTRUMENTS ARE ALL BUT USELESS. POWERLESS TO TAKE POSITIVE ACTION, THE MOOD ON THE BRIDGE IS BLEAK, ENHANCED BY COMMISSIONER FERRIS' GROWING IMPATIENCE.

In the ship's Transporter Room testing continues, using inert materials...until finally...

On Taurus II, Gaetano maintains his lonely vigil, accompanied only by a deepening depression ...until his phaser is smashed from his hand by a large rock, thrown with stunning force from somewhere in the drifting haze.

Disarmed, boxed in, Gaetano's hope vanishes with his first clear look at the shuffling, angry monstrosity advancing toward him.

Trapped, he can only face the nightmare, and wait...until his worst fears are realized... horribly.

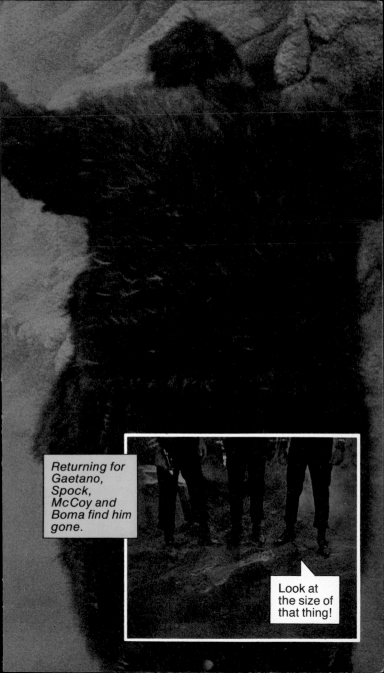

Take this back to Mr. Scott for conversion please, Doctor.

Nobody knows what's happened to Gaetano and you hand over his phaser like nothings happened at all!

And give this to Mr. Scott, in the event I don't return.

I'll do that, but just where are you going?

Venturing further into the canyon, Spock finds Gaetano's broken, lifeless body.

Easily hoisting the body to his shoulders, Spock hurries back to the Galileo.

Spock's foray to recover Gaetano's body has angered the brutes anew. His return to the ship is heralded by their loud clamor behind him.

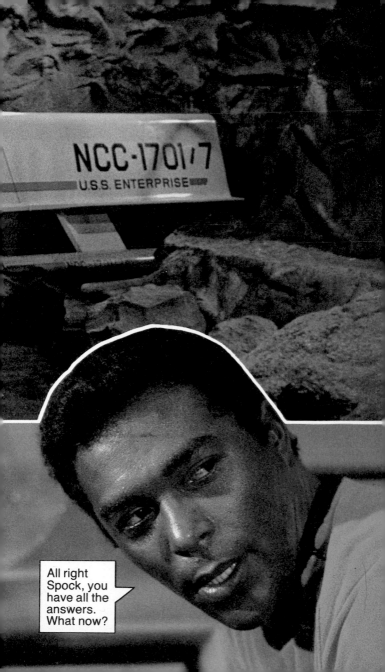

Again and again, the infuriated behemoth sends the boulder crashing into the shuttlecraft, jarring its occupants like toys in a box.

galileo

CAPTAIN'S LOG
STARDATE 2823.1

OUR LANDING PARTIES ARE
ON THE SURFACE OF TAURUS
II AND WE CONTINUE TO
HOPE. INSTRUMENTS ARE
SLOWLY RETURNING TO AN
OPERABLE CONDITION, AS
THE ION STORM SLOWLY
DISPERSES. ON THE SHIP
WE CAN ONLY WAIT HELP-
LESSLY...AS OUR TIME
RUNS OUT.

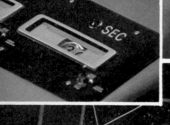

What word
from the
Sensor Section?

They're getting
some readings, sir—
partial function.

You have two
hours and forty-
three minutes,
Captain.

On Taurus II, as the pounding of the Galileo *continues, Spock conceives a plan.*

Mr. Scott, how much power do we have left in the ship's batteries?...Will they electrify the exterior of this ship?

That they will, Mr. Spock!

Everybody, get to the center of the ship! Don't touch the plates! Be sure you're insulated!

All right,
go!

Using insulated gauntlets, Engineering Officer Scott bridges the exposed contacts, enveloping the exterior of the craft in a direct charge, and eliciting an anguished response from the beast outside.

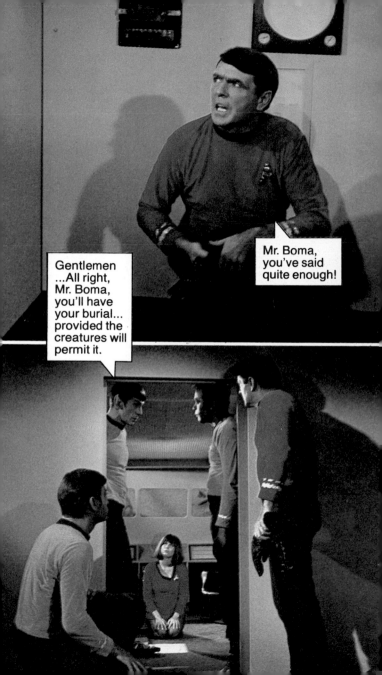

OUR TIME IS ALMOST UP. THE TRANSPORTER IS NOW FULLY OPERATIONAL, BUT WITHOUT RADIO CONTACT OR COORDINATES FOR THE "GALILEO," WE HAVE NO WAY OF BEAMING THEM UP. WE ARE AWAITING THE RETURN OF THE SEARCH PARTY ABOARD THE "COLUMBUS."

Captain Kirk, landing party number two is being beamed aboard ship. They have casualties. One dead, two injured.

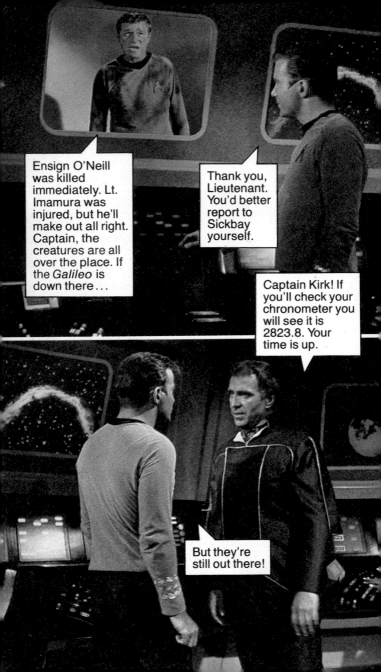

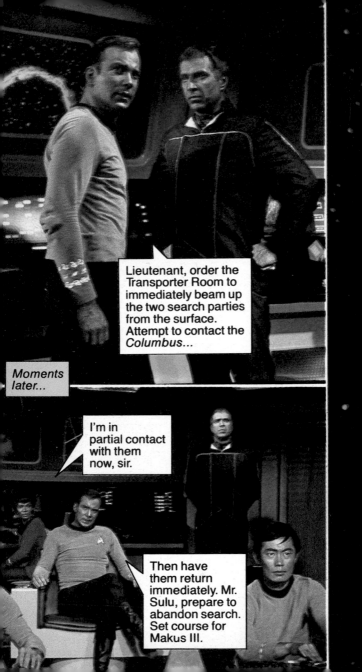

CAPTAIN'S LOG

SUPPLEMENT

THE SEARCH PARTIES
HAVE RETURNED TO THE
SHIP, AND THE "COLUM-
BUS" IS ON ITS WAY
BACK. I HAVE BEEN
COMPELLED TO
ABANDON THE SEARCH.

Twenty-three minutes, sir.
Twenty-three minutes!
And if the *Columbus* doesn't find them by then ...they won't have a prayer!

Having failed to find the *Galileo, the shuttlecraft* Columbus *returns to the hangar deck of the* Enterprise.

The *Columbus* is aboard, sir. The flight hatch is closed. Transporter Room reports the last of the landing parties have beamed safely up. All systems report secured for warp factors.

Back on Taurus II, a sudden barrage of spears and rocks interrupts the burial detail. The huge creatures are attacking in force.

Into the ship! Immediate lift-off!

McCoy and Boma check their headlong rush for the ship as Spock is pinned by a boulder thrown by the attackers.

No! No, go back... Lift off!

With all aboard aware that the time has past for the Enterprise to leave for Makus III, the little craft lifts toward orbit.

Gentlemen, by coming after me, you may well have destroyed what slim chance you had for survival. The logical thing for you to have done was to have left me behind.

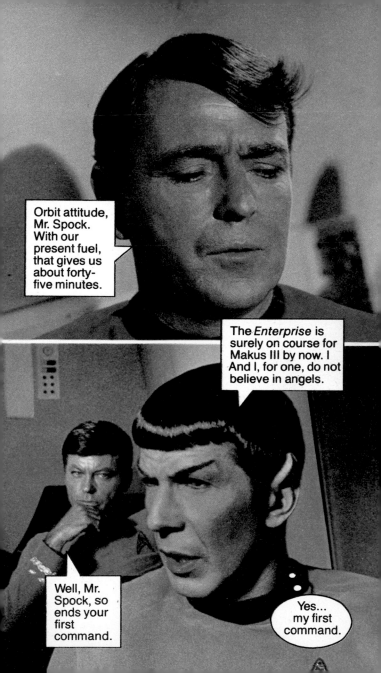

Aware that the *Enterprise* must by now be out of range for visual sighting of the tiny shuttlecraft, Spock attempts radio contact, reasoning that free of atmospheric interference, there just might be a chance.

Galileo to *Enterprise*. *Galileo* to *Enterprise!* Come in please. *Galileo* to *Enterprise...* Come in please...

There is no response. They are alone... in limited orbit over an alien, hostile planet...measuring their lives in minutes.

So **this** is how it ends...

The radio was our final alternative...**No!** ...That instrument panel... telling me... something... but **what?**

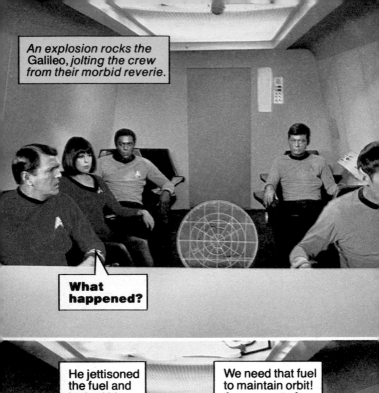

An explosion rocks the Galileo, jolting the crew from their morbid reverie.

What happened?

He jettisoned the fuel and ignited it!

We need that fuel to maintain orbit! Are you out of your mind?

Perhaps, Mr. Boma.

The Galileo *rushes toward certain burn-out, her precious fuel streaming behind her in radiant, twin plumes... like a final, futile hurrah...*

While on the Enterprise proceeding to Makus III at space-normal speed, the complex business of running the huge 190,000 metric ton starship continues, grimly...all hands now aware, via scuttlebutt, that shipmates have been left behind at Taurus II.

The mood is blackest on the bridge, where a resigned silence is broken by a shout from Helmsman Sulu...

Captain! Something there— on the screen! At Taurus II!

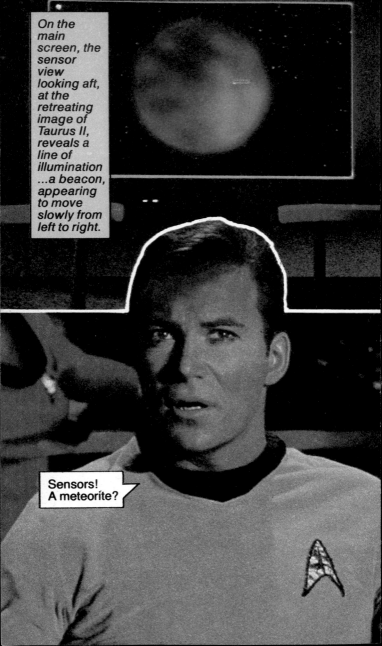

Her fuel gone, utterly doomed, the Galileo begins to burn up in the atmosphere above Taurus II.

On the bridge of the Enterprise, unable to suppress sudden hope, the mood is electric...
Transporters locked-in, sir.
Activate beams!

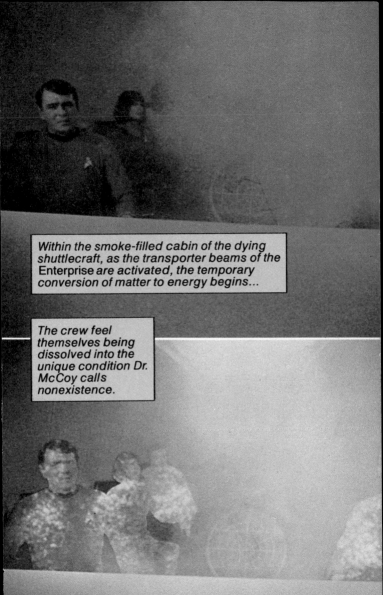

Within the smoke-filled cabin of the dying shuttlecraft, as the transporter beams of the Enterprise are activated, the temporary conversion of matter to energy begins...

The crew feel themselves being dissolved into the unique condition Dr. McCoy calls nonexistence.

GLOSSARY

Bridge—The top deck of the Starship from which the Captain, his chief officers, and the navigator control the ship.

Captain's Log—Record keeping method used by the captain of all important activities affecting the Starship.

Folsom Point—A prehistoric, finely chipped, flint point found on an archaeological dig in Folsom, New Mexico in 1925.

Ionic Interference—Atmospheric obstructions caused by charged subatomic particles.

Murasaki 312—A quasar-like formation; an electromagnetic phenomenon.

Phasers—Small hand-held weapons with several adjustable settings ranging from a mild "sting" to a fatal "kill."

Scanners—Part of the Starship's sensory machinery capable of sensing and analyzing any material surrounding the ship.

Shuttlecraft—A 24-foot long, seven passenger ship propelled by an impulse drive engine and capable of limited range intra-solar system missions.

Sickbay—A compartment in the Starship located on the seventh deck and used as a dispensary and hospital.

Space Normal Speed—Velocity less than the speed of light.

Stardate—Method of calculating time onboard the Starship.

Taurus II—An unexplored Type M planet with an oxygen/nitrogen mixture appropriate for sustaining human life.

Transporter—Used to move crew and/or cargo from the Starship to planets and back by changing the object's original molecular structure into energy which can be beamed to a predetermined point where the original molecular formation can then be reconstructed.

United Federation of Planets—Democratic alliance of planets comprised of several solar systems including Sol. All decisions affecting member planets are made through delegates to the Federation Council.

U.S.S. Enterprise—One of 13 Starships operated by the United Federation of Planets. This 190,000 metric ton craft, currently involved in a five year explorative mission, is crewed by approximately 430 people and contains, within its 11 decks, a completely self-supporting mini-city.

Viewscreens—Electronic devices positioned throughout the Starship that keep crew members in visual contact with each other. The main viewscreen is located on the ship's bridge and is capable of displaying in various magnifications all matter surrounding the ship's exterior.

Vulcans—Race inhabiting the planet Vulcan recognizable by their highly developed intelligence, pointed ears, upswept eyebrows and sallow complexion. They deny the existence of emotion and conduct their lives through logic.

Warp Drive—Method of propulsion exceeding the speed of light.